JOURNAL

This Journey belongs to:

STILL WATERS

a journey through
Lectio Divina

FOR KIDS

A DEVOTIONAL BY
SAMARA ELLEDGE

Growing with God:
A Journey Through Lectio Divina

But when the Father sends the Advocate as my representative—that is, the Holy Spirit—he will teach you everything and will remind you of everything I have told you. - Jesus
John 14:26 NLT

Lectio Divina is a bit like going on a magical journey inside your head and heart. It's a way to read and think about Bible stories, almost like you're exploring a treasure map or a book filled with secrets. Picture this: you've got a special magnifying glass, just like a detective, and you're using it to zoom in on a Bible story. First, you read a tiny part of the story. Then you start thinking about what it means and how it makes you feel, just like when you're trying to solve a mystery. After that, it's like having a heart-to-heart talk with God, sharing your thoughts and secrets, just like you would with a trusted friend. And at the end, you take a moment to be super quiet and still, just like when you're listening to the wind rustling in the trees or the soothing waves at the beach. This quiet time helps you hear what God might be saying to your heart. It's a fantastic adventure of the mind and spirit!

So, Lectio Divina is like a fun and magical way to connect with God through stories from the Bible. It's like having a special adventure with God every time you read and think about these stories, and it helps you grow closer to Him and understand His love and wisdom even better.

♡ Samara

What is Lectio Divina?

We do Lectio Divina to get even closer to God and become really good friends with Him, using stories from the Bible as our guides during our chats with Him. When we read these special stories and take quiet moments to think about them, we create a special place where God can show us how close He is and guide us on the amazing path He has for us. When we think quietly, we're inviting a super special meeting with God and a chance to discover what He wants us to do in our lives. Lectio Divina is like our special way of talking, listening, and being with God, making our friendship with Him super strong and timeless.

How do I use this journal?

QUIET

We've added this easy step to get you ready for each day's special reading time, where you can connect with God and His words. It's like taking a little break to calm your mind and heart. Close your eyes for a moment and take a deep breath. You can say a short, friendly prayer to God, like asking Him to be with you as you read His words and to help you understand and feel them in your heart. It's like saying, "Hey, God, let's read together and learn something amazing today." You can also ask Him to show you the way and be your guide, just like having a wise friend by your side.

READING (LECTIO)

The first step is like opening a treasure chest in your favorite adventure book. You read a small part of a Bible story, like when you read a page from your favorite storybook. But here, we read it very carefully, like a detective looking for hidden clues. We want to understand what's happening in the story.

REFLECTING (MEDITATIO)

After reading, it's time to think and reflect, just like when you daydream or imagine exciting adventures in your head. You ask yourself questions like, "What does this part of the story mean?" or "How would I feel if I were in the story?" It's like putting on the shoes of the characters and walking in their world. This helps us understand the story better.

RESPONDING (ORATIO)

Now, it's like having a chat with God, your best friend. You talk to God about what you read and thought. You can say things like, "God, I learned this from the story," or "Please help me with what I don't understand." It's like sharing your secrets and feelings with God. You can also ask for guidance or help if you need it.

RESTING (CONTEMPLATIO)

In the last step, it's time to be very still and quiet. It's like when you sit silently in a peaceful garden and listen to the birds sing. You give your heart a chance to listen to what God might want to tell you. Sometimes, God speaks softly in your heart, and in this quiet moment, you can hear Him better. It's like a calm, peaceful time with your best friend, God.

So, that's how Lectio Divina works! It's like going on a special adventure with God through the Bible, step by step, like reading a treasure map to find hidden treasures of wisdom and love.

weekly Examen:
A Reflection upon your week

Imagine having a special superpower that helps you see all the wonderful things that happened in your week and feel even closer to God. That's what the Weekly Examen is all about! It's like a magical review of your week, where you can discover God's love and guidance in everything you do. So, once a week, let's embark on this exciting adventure of prayerful reflection together!

STEP 1: FIND A QUIET MOMENT

Set aside some quiet time at the end of your week when you won't be interrupted. Find a comfy and peaceful spot. It's like creating a cozy corner for your heart-to-heart talk with God.

This is also a great practice for your family to do together once a week. Ask your parents to help set aside a time that you can all do this together. Maybe during or after dinner one night each week.

STEP 2: GIVE THANKS TO GOD

Think about all of the things that made you happy during the week, like fun moments, delicious treats, or friendly smiles. Thank God for these special times, just like saying 'Thank you' for a surprise gift. It's like counting your blessings and sharing your joy with God.

STEP 3: REFLECT ON YOUR WEEK

Picture your entire week like a big slideshow in your mind. Ask God to help you remember what happened, from Monday to now. It's like watching a special movie together with God, and He'll help you see things you might have missed.

STEP 4: SHARE YOUR FEELINGS WITH GOD

Now, think about how you felt during those moments in your week. Were you happy, sad, or maybe a bit puzzled? Share those feelings with God, like chatting with a friend about your week. God is a great listener, and He cares about how you feel.

STEP 5: SAY SORRY AND ASK FOR HELP

If you remember any times when you made a mistake or wished you did things differently, don't worry. We all make mistakes sometimes. Tell God you're sorry, just like saying 'I'm sorry' to a friend when you make a mistake. Ask God for help to do better next time.

STEP 6: LOOK AHEAD WITH GOD

Think about the upcoming week and all the adventures it might bring. Ask God to be with you and guide you, just like a captain steering a ship. You're getting ready for a new week with God by your side.

This Weekly Examen is like a special time to chat with God about your week. It helps you feel closer to Him and learn more about yourself. So, give it a try and discover how wonderful it can be!

TIME TO BRAINSTORM

Now that you know what the Weekly Examen looks like. Brainstorm some times during the week that you could try to add this into your day. Some possible options are:

- ♥ during a weekend dinner
- ♥ Sunday afternoon
- ♥ after dinner
- ♥ with a fun Saturday morning breakfast

What are some times that you could fit this in during your week? If you are going to do this together with your family, ask them to help with sharing some ideas of when to do this.

_____

_____

_____

_____

_____

_____

_____

Discovering the Magic of Journaling: Growing Closer to Yourself and God

In the special practice of Lectio Divina, journaling becomes your trusted friend, helping you explore your feelings and connect with God. Writing down what you read in the Bible and how it makes you feel is like a special way to be mindful. It asks you to slow down, listen carefully, and think deeply, helping you understand yourself better, which is super important for growing as a person. Your journal isn't just for writing; it's like a magical bridge that connects you with God. When you put your thoughts, ideas, and prayers on its pages, you're bringing together the human and the divine. Your journal becomes a special place where your private thoughts and the wisdom of the Bible come together, showing you how you're growing spiritually and reminding you that God is always there with you, just like a warm hug in the pages of your journal.

You'll find special pages in your journal just for you to write and think about your journey. You can let your thoughts flow freely, turn a verse into a prayer, or make a list of things that bother you and you want to talk to God about. Use these pages however you like, depending on what feels right for you at that time.

Drawing for Self-Discovery: Finding Inner Calm

Imagine if you had a magic wand that could take you to a peaceful world where you could relax, have fun, and discover amazing things about yourself. Well, guess what? You have something even better – your imagination and the power of art! Meditative drawing is like a magical journey where you can use colors and lines to create beautiful pictures and, at the same time, find calmness inside yourself. It's like having a secret language between your heart and your paper, where you can express your feelings and thoughts. So, let's dive into the world of meditative drawing, where you can unwind, be creative, and learn more about the wonderful person you are!

Don't feel like drawing?

Sometimes, you might think, 'I'm not very good at drawing or painting, so maybe I shouldn't even try.' But guess what? Art isn't about being perfect; it's about expressing yourself and having fun. Think about learning to ride a bike or trying out a new topic in school; that can be tricky. Art might seem a bit tricky at first too. But here's a secret: everyone starts from somewhere, and even those artists you admire so much were once beginners too! So, don't hesitate to pick up that pencil or paintbrush. Your art is just like a fingerprint – unique and super special. It's your way of showing the world who you are. And who knows, you might uncover talents you didn't even know you had. So, let's give it a whirl together and see where your creativity leads you. You could end up surprising yourself with the fantastic things you can create!

Exploring Your Creative Path: Fun Art Prompts and Coloring Adventures

If you ever feel a little unsure about your art skills, don't worry! We're here to support you every step of the way. Inside this journal, you'll find not just empty pages but also fun coloring pictures and special art ideas meant to light up your creative spirit. Think of these resources as friendly helpers, like having buddies along for your meditative drawing adventure. They'll inspire your artistic journey and show you where to start when you're not sure. But remember, there are no rules here, only an invitation to enjoy expressing yourself and feel calm while you let your creativity flow. So, take a deep breath, grab your colors, and let your inner artist shine, one stroke at a time.

Serene Sketches:
Finding Peace Through Relaxing Sketches

We made Serene Sketches to be a peaceful place for you to relax your mind and add a touch of tranquility to your everyday life with art. This special program is made just for you, and it's all about using soothing sketches to help you find your inner calm and learn more about yourself. With patterns that repeat and mindful creativity, we want to show you how to feel super peaceful and bring that peace into everything you do. As you doodle and draw lines and shapes on paper, you're not only unlocking your artistic talents but also opening the door to a sense of calm and quiet that can help you handle life's challenges gracefully. Come with us on this art adventure, where sketching becomes a way to find peace and balance, and connect with the calm beauty inside all of us.

Getting Ready

Start by gathering your doodling tools - like a clean sheet of paper or a special doodle book, fine-tipped markers or pens in different sizes, and a comfy, quiet place. Take a few deep breaths to center yourself and get ready for a relaxing time.

Pick Your Patterns

Choose three or four simple patterns that you like and can easily repeat. These could be waves, spirals, dots, or lines. You can even make up your patterns if you want. The important thing is that they're easy to draw again and again without much trouble.

Begin with a Center

Right in the middle of your paper, draw a small shape or design. This is the most important part of your drawing and what you'll focus on. It can be anything you like, like a circle, a flower, or even a star.

Let the Patterns Flow

Start by choosing one of your patterns. Begin drawing it from your centerpiece in a circular or ring-like way. Don't worry if it's not perfect; the idea is to create a sense of flow and repetition.

Mix Up the Patterns

While you keep going with your first pattern, you can introduce another one into your drawing. For example, if you start with waves, you can add dots or spirals between the waves. Let them mix and match naturally.

Trust Your Feelings

As you doodle, let your feelings guide you. There's no right or wrong way to put patterns together. This is all about being in the moment and letting your creativity go without any rules.

Keep Going

Keep expanding your design, adding more patterns as you go. Slowly fill up a small space or the whole page; stop when it feels right to you. Remember, this is a relaxing journey, so take your time and enjoy it.

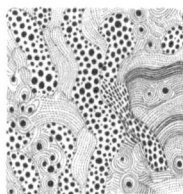

Add Some Color (If You Want)

If you'd like, you can make your doodle even more colorful. Use colored markers, pencils, or watercolors to make your creation look even more exciting.

Relax and Have Fun

Remember, the Serene Sketches process is meant to be enjoyable and flexible. Take all the time you need; there's no rush. If it ever starts to feel stressful or you're trying too hard for it to be perfect, gently put it down. You can choose to work on just a part of the page or fill the whole thing - whatever feels best for you at that moment. The main idea here is to find joy and peace through your creativity, so don't worry about being perfect and let your doodles flow naturally.

Reflect and Record

Once you've completed your Serene Sketch, find a quiet moment to sit and ponder how it made you feel. Write down all those thoughts and feelings in your journal. This will make your connection with doodling even stronger.

Keep Doing It

To get the most out of your doodling with many patterns, try to make it a regular thing. Set aside time every day or week to create new designs and combinations. Over time, you'll see that this creative practice not only brings you peace but also improves your artistic skills and self-awareness.

Pattern Ideas

At the end of the journal, we've provided some pages of pattern ideas for you to use during your Serene Sketches process. You can use these to spur on your creative process in doodling. Some other ideas are to search patterns in books and magazines or have your parents help you find some on the internet. We also love to search artists on Instagram and pinterest for fun ideas, so you can ask your parents for help with that too.

Enjoy the process, have fun and just try different patterns together and see what ends up on the page!

"Good artists copy, great artists steal" - attributed to Pablo Picasso

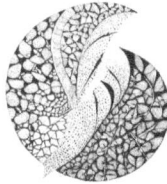

From Reflection to Action:
Translating Lectio Divina Insights into Daily Practice

The journey of Lectio Divina is like a special adventure where you explore your thoughts and connect with God. But the real magic happens when you use what you've learned in your everyday life. As you read and think about sacred words, here are some ideas to help you turn those lessons into actions that can make the world a better place:

Volunteer

Spread love and kindness by dedicating your time and skills to a cause that holds meaning for you. Consider how your Lectio Divina insights can guide your volunteer work. You, along with your family, can make a difference at your church, help a charity, lend a hand at a community event, or be part of a social project. Remember, when you help others, it's like showing your love for God. Your acts of kindness reveal the care and empathy you've nurtured through practices like Lectio Divina.

"Truly I tell you, whatever you did for one of the least of these brothers and sisters of mine, you did for me." Matthew 25:40 (NIV)

Give

Practice being generous by giving to others in ways that feel right to you. You can give to your church, donate to a charity you believe in, share your skills to help someone in need, or simply be a good friend. Ask God to guide you in finding new ways to be generous. Your actions should come from a place of love and a desire to help others, just like God wants us to give with a joyful heart.

"Each of you should give what you have decided in your heart to give, not reluctantly or under compulsion, for God loves a cheerful giver." 2 Corinthians 9:7 (NIV)

Share What You've Learned

The wisdom you've gained from Lectio Divina can inspire others. Share your thoughts, experiences, and what you've learned with your friends, family, or online communities. By doing this, you spread the positive energy of divine reading to others who might find it helpful.

"As iron sharpens iron, so one person sharpens another." Proverbs 27:17 (NIV)

Connect with Friends

Sometimes, we forget that our friends may need our help and support too. Have heart-to-heart talks with your friends and use what you've learned in Lectio Divina to guide your conversations. By sharing your reflections and inviting them to share theirs, you can both grow and strengthen your friendship.

"Perfume and incense bring joy to the heart, and the pleasantness of a friend springs from their heartfelt advice." Proverbs 27:9 (NIV)

Inspire Someone

Let the wisdom you've gained from Lectio Divina be a source of inspiration for those around you. Whether it's through your actions, words, or creative projects, try to uplift and motivate someone in your life. By sharing Jesus' love, you can make a positive impact on others.

"Do nothing out of selfish ambition or vain conceit. Rather, in humility value others above yourselves, not looking to your own interests but each of you to the interests of the others." Philippians 2:3-4 (NIV)

As you think about these ideas and take steps to put your Lectio Divina lessons into action, you'll bring more meaning and compassion into your daily life. Each action becomes a way to show how reflection, God's plan, and real change are all connected, making the world a kinder and more thoughtful place to live.

Starting your Journey

Welcome to an amazing adventure called Lectio Divina! It's a journey of discovering more about yourself, connecting with God, and growing into a better you. We're super excited that you're joining us on this adventure. It's time to move into action and spend some time reading the Bible and talking and listening to God. So, with a happy heart and a curious mind, let's start this incredible adventure and see all the cool stuff God has for us!

Quiet

Date:__/__/____

Prepare for today's Bible reading with a few moments of quieting your mind

Reading Isaiah 40:8

Read the Scripture out loud slowly, listening & creating space for the words. Repeat up to 3x.

Reflecting

Choose a word, phrase, or concept that speaks to you and write these down.
What does this part of the story mean? How would I feel if I were in the story?

_____

_____

_____

_____

Responding

Talk to God about what you read. You can ask God for guidance or help if you need it. You can also write out your prayer.

_____

_____

_____

_____

Resting

Rest in God's love while being still and quiet. Listen to what God wants to tell you.

Art & Prayer

Welcome, creative explorers! Today is a special day just for you to dive into the world of meditative art and connect with God through your creativity. Get ready to relax, have fun, and let your imagination soar as we embark on this artistic adventure together. Grab your art supplies, find a comfy spot, and let's begin our creative journey!

Today you have a coloring page if you would like to color. You also have the rest of this page to draw or sketch anything that comes to mind. You could even write out a prayer to God and then color, draw or sketch around it! Have fun!

Memory Verse

Today you are going to take a look at our verse of the week and spend some time committing it to your heart. Spend your time today memorizing this verse. Try to recite it several times throughout the day. It's okay to look at it again if you can't quite remember it all.

Challenge: Can you recite it to a parent, teacher, or friend?

It helps to write out the verse as you are memorizing it. Take some time to rewrite the verse. You can even write it on a sticky note so you can place it somewhere to see it throughout the day, like on your mirror or on the fridge.

The grass withers and the flowers fade,
but the word of our God stands forever.
Isaiah 40:8 NLT

_____

_____

_____

_____

_____

_____

_____

_____

_____

_____

Gratitude

Hey there, young gratitude champions! Today is all about celebrating the good stuff in our lives. Take a moment to think about the week that's passed and jot down 3-4 things that made you smile, feel warm inside, or just plain happy. It could be something big or teeny-tiny, like a friend's laugh, a tasty treat, a sunny day, or a cozy book. By counting our blessings, we remind ourselves of all the awesome things that fill our days with joy and how amazing God is.

So, in the space below, write down what you are thankful for this week!

And if there is someone you are grateful for on your list: Go and Tell them!

The grass withers and the flowers fade,
but the word of our God stands forever.
Isaiah 40:8 NLT

_____

_____

_____

_____

_____

_____

_____

_____

_____

_____

_____

Write Your Prayer

Dear young prayer warriors, today is a special day to connect with God through your words and feelings. You can write a prayer using the Bible verse we've been exploring this week, or simply share what's on your heart today. It's a chance to talk to God about anything and everything – your worries, what's making you sad, the things you're struggling with, and even your joys and praises. Your words are like a bridge that brings you closer to God, so write in the space below and let your heart speak through your prayers.

The grass withers and the flowers fade,
but the word of our God stands forever.
Isaiah 40:8 NLT

_____

_____

_____

_____

_____

_____

_____

_____

_____

_____

_____

_____

weekly Examen Prayer   Date:__/__/____

Step 1: Find a Quiet Moment

Set aside some quiet time at the end of your week when you won't be interrupted. Find a comfy and peaceful spot. It's like creating a cozy corner for your heart-to-heart talk with God.

Step 2: Give Thanks to God

Think about all of the things that made you happy during the week, like fun moments, delicious treats, or friendly smiles. Thank God for these special times, just like saying 'Thank you' for a surprise gift. It's like counting your blessings and sharing your joy with God.

Step 3: Reflect on Your Week

Picture your entire week like a big slideshow in your mind. Ask God to help you remember what happened, from Monday to now. It's like watching a special movie together with God, and He'll help you see things you might have missed.

Step 4: Share Your Feelings with God

Now, think about how you felt during those moments in your week. Were you happy, sad, or maybe a bit puzzled? Share those feelings with God, like chatting with a friend about your week. God is a great listener, and He cares about how you feel.

Step 5: Say Sorry and Ask for Help

If you remember any times when you made a mistake or wished you did things differently, don't worry. We all make mistakes sometimes. Tell God you're sorry, just like saying 'I'm sorry' to a friend when you make a mistake. Ask God for help to do better next time.

weekly Examen Prayer

Date:___/___/_____

Step 6: Look Ahead with God

Think about the upcoming week and all the adventures it might bring. Ask God to be with you and guide you, just like a captain steering a ship. You're getting ready for a new week with God by your side.

This Weekly Examen is like a special time to chat with God about your week. It helps you feel closer to Him and learn more about yourself. So, give it a try and discover how wonderful it can be!

Use the space below to write down anything that God shared with you during this time or anything that you would like to remember from this week's experiences.

_____

_____

_____

_____

_____

_____

_____

_____

_____

_____

_____

Day of Rest & Fun

Date:___/___/_____

Do you remember what God did on the seventh day? Yes! He rested. That could mean a nap, or maybe He did something that filled him, like playing a game, or reading a good book. Can you imagine that? God reading a book? Fun!

Today is a day of rest and fun. Listed below are some options for you to choose from or you can come up with some of your own and write them down! Be creative, spend some time with your family, and make some fun memories!

1. Art and Craft Day: Get creative with drawing, painting, or crafting. You can make colorful cards, friendship bracelets, or even paint a picture of your favorite animal.

2. Baking or Cooking: Try baking cookies, making your own pizza, or preparing a special family recipe. Don't forget to enjoy the tasty results together!

3. Nature Scavenger Hunt: Go on a nature scavenger hunt in your backyard or at a nearby park. Make a list of things to find, like pinecones, different leaves, or animal tracks.

4. Picnic in the Park: Pack a picnic basket with sandwiches, fruit, and snacks, and head to the park for a delicious outdoor meal with your family or friends.

What are some ideas you can come up with? Choose one to do today:

_____

_____

_____

_____

Journal

You can let your thoughts flow freely, turn a verse into a prayer, or make a list of things that bother you and you want to talk to God about.
Use this page however you like.

_____

_____

_____

_____

_____

_____

_____

_____

_____

_____

_____

_____

_____

_____

_____

_____

Quiet

Date:___/___/_____

Prepare for today's Bible reading with a few moments of quieting your mind

Reading Psalm 73:24-25

Read the Scripture out loud slowly, listening & creating space for the words. Repeat up to 3x.

Reflecting

Choose a word, phrase, or concept that speaks to you and write these down. What does this part of the story mean? How would I feel if I were in the story?

_____

_____

_____

_____

_____

Responding

Talk to God about what you read. You can ask God for guidance or help if you need it. You can also write out your prayer.

_____

_____

_____

_____

_____

_____

Resting

Rest in God's love while being still and quiet. Listen to what God wants to tell you.

Art & Prayer

Welcome, creative explorers! Today is a special day just for you to dive into the world of meditative art and connect with God through your creativity. Get ready to relax, have fun, and let your imagination soar as we embark on this artistic adventure together. Grab your art supplies, find a comfy spot, and let's begin our creative journey!

Are you ready to try your own Serene Sketch? There are some pattern ideas on the next page for you to play around with.

You have the rest of this page to draw or sketch anything that comes to mind. You could even write out a prayer to God and then color, draw or sketch around it! Have fun!

PatternIdeas

Select 2-4 patterns to create your own meditative artwork piece:

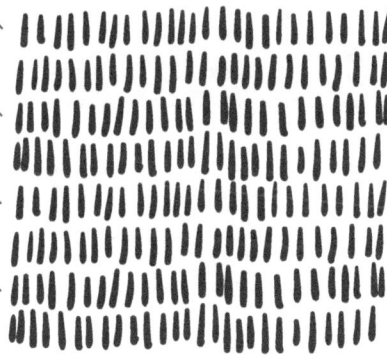

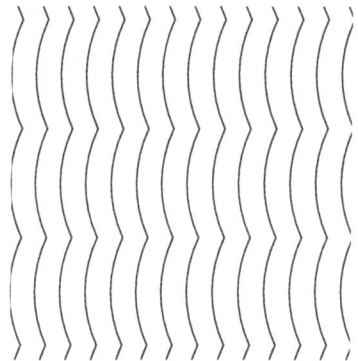

Memory Verse

Today you are going to take a look at our verse of the week and spend some time committing it to your heart. Spend your time today memorizing this verse. Try to recite it several times throughout the day. It's okay to look at it again if you can't quite remember it all.

Challenge: Can you recite it to a parent, teacher, or friend?

It helps to write out the verse as you are memorizing it. Take some time to rewrite the verse. You can even write it on a sticky note so you can place it somewhere to see it throughout the day, like on your mirror or on the fridge.

> You guide me with your counsel,
>   leading me to a glorious destiny.
>   Whom have I in heaven but you?
>   I desire you more than anything on earth.
>   Psalm 73:24-25 NLT

_____

_____

_____

_____

_____

_____

_____

_____

Gratitude

Hey there, young gratitude champions! Today is all about celebrating the good stuff in our lives. Take a moment to think about the week that's passed and jot down 3-4 things that made you smile, feel warm inside, or just plain happy. It could be something big or teeny-tiny, like a friend's laugh, a tasty treat, a sunny day, or a cozy book. By counting our blessings, we remind ourselves of all the awesome things that fill our days with joy and how amazing God is.

So, in the space below, write down what you are thankful for this week!

And if there is someone you are grateful for on your list: Go and Tell them!

You guide me with your counsel,
leading me to a glorious destiny.
Whom have I in heaven but you?
I desire you more than anything on earth.
Psalm 73:24-25 NLT

_____

_____

_____

_____

_____

_____

_____

_____

_____

_____

Write Your Prayer

Date:__/__/____

Dear young prayer warriors, today is a special day to connect with God through your words and feelings. You can write a prayer using the Bible verse we've been exploring this week, or simply share what's on your heart today. It's a chance to talk to God about anything and everything – your worries, what's making you sad, the things you're struggling with, and even your joys and praises. Your words are like a bridge that brings you closer to God, so write in the space below and let your heart speak through your prayers.

> You guide me with your counsel,
> leading me to a glorious destiny.
> Whom have I in heaven but you?
> I desire you more than anything on earth.
> Psalm 73:24-25 NLT

_____

_____

_____

_____

_____

_____

_____

_____

_____

_____

_____

weekly Examen Prayer

Date:___/___/_____

Step 1: Find a Quiet Moment

Set aside some quiet time at the end of your week when you won't be interrupted. Find a comfy and peaceful spot. It's like creating a cozy corner for your heart-to-heart talk with God.

Step 2: Give Thanks to God

Think about all of the things that made you happy during the week, like fun moments, delicious treats, or friendly smiles. Thank God for these special times, just like saying 'Thank you' for a surprise gift. It's like counting your blessings and sharing your joy with God.

Step 3: Reflect on Your Week

Picture your entire week like a big slideshow in your mind. Ask God to help you remember what happened, from Monday to now. It's like watching a special movie together with God, and He'll help you see things you might have missed.

Step 4: Share Your Feelings with God

Now, think about how you felt during those moments in your week. Were you happy, sad, or maybe a bit puzzled? Share those feelings with God, like chatting with a friend about your week. God is a great listener, and He cares about how you feel.

Step 5: Say Sorry and Ask for Help

If you remember any times when you made a mistake or wished you did things differently, don't worry. We all make mistakes sometimes. Tell God you're sorry, just like saying 'I'm sorry' to a friend when you make a mistake. Ask God for help to do better next time.

weekly Examen Prayer

Date:___/___/____

Step 6: Look Ahead with God

Think about the upcoming week and all the adventures it might bring. Ask God to be with you and guide you, just like a captain steering a ship. You're getting ready for a new week with God by your side.

This Weekly Examen is like a special time to chat with God about your week. It helps you feel closer to Him and learn more about yourself. So, give it a try and discover how wonderful it can be!

Use the space below to write down anything that God shared with you during this time or anything that you would like to remember from this week's experiences.

_____

_____

_____

_____

_____

_____

_____

_____

_____

_____

_____

Day of Rest & Fun

Date:___/___/____

Do you remember what God did on the seventh day? Yes! He rested. That could mean a nap, or maybe He did something that filled him, like playing a game, or reading a good book. Can you imagine that? God reading a book? Fun!

Today is a day of rest and fun. Listed below are some options for you to choose from or you can come up with some of your own and write them down! Be creative, spend some time with your family, and make some fun memories!

1. Board Games and Puzzles: Have a board game marathon with family or friends. Puzzles and board games like Scrabble, Monopoly, or Uno can be loads of fun.

2. Movie or Book Marathon: Pick a series of books or movies and spend the day reading or watching them. Create a cozy reading nook or have a movie marathon with popcorn.

3. Bike Ride or Scooter Adventure: Take a bike ride or scooter adventure around your neighborhood or on a nearby trail. Don't forget your helmet!

4. Cook or Bake Together: Prepare a meal or dessert as a family team. Everyone can have a role, from chopping vegetables to setting the table.

What are some ideas you can come up with? Choose one to do today:

_____

_____

_____

_____

Journal

You can let your thoughts flow freely, turn a verse into a prayer, or make a list of things that bother you and you want to talk to God about.
Use this page however you like.

_____

_____

_____

_____

_____

_____

_____

_____

_____

_____

_____

_____

_____

_____

_____

Quiet

Date:___/___/____

Prepare for today's Bible reading with a few moments of quieting your mind

Reading 2 Timothy 1:7

Read the Scripture out loud slowly, listening & creating space for the words. Repeat up to 3x.

Reflecting

Choose a word, phrase, or concept that speaks to you and write these down. What does this part of the story mean? How would I feel if I were in the story?

_____

_____

_____

_____

_____

Responding

Talk to God about what you read. You can ask God for guidance or help if you need it. You can also write out your prayer.

_____

_____

_____

_____

_____

Resting

Rest in God's love while being still and quiet. Listen to what God wants to tell you.

Art & Prayer

Welcome, creative explorers! Today is a special day just for you to dive into the world of meditative art and connect with God through your creativity. Get ready to relax, have fun, and let your imagination soar as we embark on this artistic adventure together. Grab your art supplies, find a comfy spot, and let's begin our creative journey!

Today you have a coloring page if you would like to color. You also have the rest of this page to draw or sketch anything that comes to mind. You could even write out a prayer to God and then color, draw or sketch around it! Have fun!

Memory Verse

Today you are going to take a look at our verse of the week and spend some time committing it to your heart. Spend your time today memorizing this verse. Try to recite it several times throughout the day. It's okay to look at it again if you can't quite remember it all.

Challenge: Can you recite it to a parent, teacher, or friend?

It helps to write out the verse as you are memorizing it. Take some time to rewrite the verse. You can even write it on a sticky note so you can place it somewhere to see it throughout the day, like on your mirror or on the fridge.

For God has not given us a spirit of fear and timidity,
but of power, love, and self-discipline.
2 Timothy 1:7 NLT

_____

_____

_____

_____

_____

_____

_____

_____

_____

_____

Gratitude

Hey there, young gratitude champions! Today is all about celebrating the good stuff in our lives. Take a moment to think about the week that's passed and jot down 3-4 things that made you smile, feel warm inside, or just plain happy. It could be something big or teeny-tiny, like a friend's laugh, a tasty treat, a sunny day, or a cozy book. By counting our blessings, we remind ourselves of all the awesome things that fill our days with joy and how amazing God is.

So, in the space below, write down what you are thankful for this week!

And if there is someone you are grateful for on your list: Go and Tell them!

For God has not given us a spirit of fear and timidity,
but of power, love, and self-discipline.
2 Timothy 1:7 NLT

_____

_____

_____

_____

_____

_____

_____

_____

_____

Write Your Prayer

Date:___/___/____

Dear young prayer warriors, today is a special day to connect with God through your words and feelings. You can write a prayer using the Bible verse we've been exploring this week, or simply share what's on your heart today. It's a chance to talk to God about anything and everything – your worries, what's making you sad, the things you're struggling with, and even your joys and praises. Your words are like a bridge that brings you closer to God, so write in the space below and let your heart speak through your prayers.

For God has not given us a spirit of fear and timidity,
but of power, love, and self-discipline.
2 Timothy 1:7 NLT

_____

_____

_____

_____

_____

_____

_____

_____

_____

_____

_____

weekly Examen Prayer   Date:__/__/____

Step 1: Find a Quiet Moment

Set aside some quiet time at the end of your week when you won't be interrupted. Find a comfy and peaceful spot. It's like creating a cozy corner for your heart-to-heart talk with God.

Step 2: Give Thanks to God

Think about all of the things that made you happy during the week, like fun moments, delicious treats, or friendly smiles. Thank God for these special times, just like saying 'Thank you' for a surprise gift. It's like counting your blessings and sharing your joy with God.

Step 3: Reflect on Your Week

Picture your entire week like a big slideshow in your mind. Ask God to help you remember what happened, from Monday to now. It's like watching a special movie together with God, and He'll help you see things you might have missed.

Step 4: Share Your Feelings with God

Now, think about how you felt during those moments in your week. Were you happy, sad, or maybe a bit puzzled? Share those feelings with God, like chatting with a friend about your week. God is a great listener, and He cares about how you feel.

Step 5: Say Sorry and Ask for Help

If you remember any times when you made a mistake or wished you did things differently, don't worry. We all make mistakes sometimes. Tell God you're sorry, just like saying 'I'm sorry' to a friend when you make a mistake. Ask God for help to do better next time.

weekly Examen Prayer

Date:__/__/___

Step 6: Look Ahead with God

Think about the upcoming week and all the adventures it might bring. Ask God to be with you and guide you, just like a captain steering a ship. You're getting ready for a new week with God by your side.

This Weekly Examen is like a special time to chat with God about your week. It helps you feel closer to Him and learn more about yourself. So, give it a try and discover how wonderful it can be!

Use the space below to write down anything that God shared with you during this time or anything that you would like to remember from this week's experiences.

_____

_____

_____

_____

_____

_____

_____

_____

_____

_____

_____

Day of Rest & Fun

Date:__/__/____

Do you remember what God did on the seventh day? Yes! He rested. That could mean a nap, or maybe He did something that filled him, like playing a game, or reading a good book. Can you imagine that? God reading a book? Fun!

Today is a day of rest and fun. Listed below are some options for you to choose from or you can come up with some of your own and write them down! Be creative, spend some time with your family, and make some fun memories!

1. Science Experiments: Conduct simple science experiments at home. You can make a volcano, create a rainbow with a glass of water, or even make slime.

2. Plant a Garden: Start a small garden in your backyard or on your windowsill. You can grow flowers, herbs, or even vegetables. Watching them grow can be very exciting!

3. Sidewalk Chalk Art: Grab some colorful sidewalk chalk and create beautiful artwork on your driveway or sidewalk. You can draw hopscotch, write positive messages, or create colorful designs.

4. Family Game Day: Invite your family to play games together. Whether it's a classic board game, a card game, or charades, it's a great way to bond.

What are some ideas you can come up with? Choose one to do today:

_____

_____

_____

_____

Journal

You can let your thoughts flow freely, turn a verse into a prayer, or make a list of things that bother you and you want to talk to God about.
Use this page however you like.

_____

_____

_____

_____

_____

_____

_____

_____

_____

_____

_____

_____

_____

_____

_____

_____

Quiet

Date:___/___/____

Prepare for today's Bible reading with a few moments of quieting your mind

Reading James 1:17

Read the Scripture out loud slowly, listening & creating space for the words. Repeat up to 3x.

Reflecting

Choose a word, phrase, or concept that speaks to you and write these down. What does this part of the story mean? How would I feel if I were in the story?

_____

_____

_____

_____

_____

Responding

Talk to God about what you read. You can ask God for guidance or help if you need it. You can also write out your prayer.

_____

_____

_____

_____

_____

Resting

Rest in God's love while being still and quiet. Listen to what God wants to tell you.

Art & Prayer

Welcome, creative explorers! Today is a special day just for you to dive into the world of meditative art and connect with God through your creativity. Get ready to relax, have fun, and let your imagination soar as we embark on this artistic adventure together. Grab your art supplies, find a comfy spot, and let's begin our creative journey!

Are you ready to try your own Serene Sketch? There are some pattern ideas on the next page for you to play around with.

You have the rest of this page to draw or sketch anything that comes to mind. You could even write out a prayer to God and then color, draw or sketch around it! Have fun!

PatternIdeas

Select 2-4 patterns to create your own meditative artwork piece:

Memory Verse

Today you are going to take a look at our verse of the week and spend some time committing it to your heart. Spend your time today memorizing this verse. Try to recite it several times throughout the day. It's okay to look at it again if you can't quite remember it all.

Challenge: Can you recite it to a parent, teacher, or friend?

It helps to write out the verse as you are memorizing it. Take some time to rewrite the verse. You can even write it on a sticky note so you can place it somewhere to see it throughout the day, like on your mirror or on the fridge.

> Whatever is good and perfect is a gift coming down to
> us from God our Father, who created all the lights in
> the heavens.
> He never changes or casts a shifting shadow.
> James 1:17 NLT

_____

_____

_____

_____

_____

_____

_____

_____

_____

_____

Gratitude

Hey there, young gratitude champions! Today is all about celebrating the good stuff in our lives. Take a moment to think about the week that's passed and jot down 3-4 things that made you smile, feel warm inside, or just plain happy. It could be something big or teeny-tiny, like a friend's laugh, a tasty treat, a sunny day, or a cozy book. By counting our blessings, we remind ourselves of all the awesome things that fill our days with joy and how amazing God is.

So, in the space below, write down what you are thankful for this week!

And if there is someone you are grateful for on your list: Go and Tell them!

Whatever is good and perfect is a gift coming down to
us from God our Father, who created all the lights in
the heavens.
He never changes or casts a shifting shadow.
James 1:17 NLT

_____

_____

_____

_____

_____

_____

_____

_____

_____

Write Your Prayer

Date:___/___/____

Dear young prayer warriors, today is a special day to connect with God through your words and feelings. You can write a prayer using the Bible verse we've been exploring this week, or simply share what's on your heart today. It's a chance to talk to God about anything and everything – your worries, what's making you sad, the things you're struggling with, and even your joys and praises. Your words are like a bridge that brings you closer to God, so write in the space below and let your heart speak through your prayers.

Whatever is good and perfect is a gift coming down to
us from God our Father, who created all the lights in
the heavens.
He never changes or casts a shifting shadow.
James 1:17 NLT

_____

_____

_____

_____

_____

_____

_____

_____

_____

_____

_____

Weekly Examen Prayer
Date:__/__/____

Step 1: Find a Quiet Moment

Set aside some quiet time at the end of your week when you won't be interrupted. Find a comfy and peaceful spot. It's like creating a cozy corner for your heart-to-heart talk with God.

Step 2: Give Thanks to God

Think about all of the things that made you happy during the week, like fun moments, delicious treats, or friendly smiles. Thank God for these special times, just like saying 'Thank you' for a surprise gift. It's like counting your blessings and sharing your joy with God.

Step 3: Reflect on Your Week

Picture your entire week like a big slideshow in your mind. Ask God to help you remember what happened, from Monday to now. It's like watching a special movie together with God, and He'll help you see things you might have missed.

Step 4: Share Your Feelings with God

Now, think about how you felt during those moments in your week. Were you happy, sad, or maybe a bit puzzled? Share those feelings with God, like chatting with a friend about your week. God is a great listener, and He cares about how you feel.

Step 5: Say Sorry and Ask for Help

If you remember any times when you made a mistake or wished you did things differently, don't worry. We all make mistakes sometimes. Tell God you're sorry, just like saying 'I'm sorry' to a friend when you make a mistake. Ask God for help to do better next time.

weekly Examen Prayer

Date: __/__/___

Step 6: Look Ahead with God

Think about the upcoming week and all the adventures it might bring. Ask God to be with you and guide you, just like a captain steering a ship. You're getting ready for a new week with God by your side.

This Weekly Examen is like a special time to chat with God about your week. It helps you feel closer to Him and learn more about yourself. So, give it a try and discover how wonderful it can be!

Use the space below to write down anything that God shared with you during this time or anything that you would like to remember from this week's experiences.

_____

_____

_____

_____

_____

_____

_____

_____

_____

_____

_____

Day of Rest & Fun

Date:__/__/___

Do you remember what God did on the seventh day? Yes! He rested. That could mean a nap, or maybe He did something that filled him, like playing a game, or reading a good book. Can you imagine that? God reading a book? Fun!

Today is a day of rest and fun. Listed below are some options for you to choose from or you can come up with some of your own and write them down! Be creative, spend some time with your family, and make some fun memories!

1. Visit a Museum or Zoo: Explore a local museum, science center, or zoo with your family. It's a fantastic way to learn and have fun together.

2. Hiking or Nature Walk: Plan a family hike in a nearby nature reserve or forest. Bring a backpack with snacks and enjoy the beauty of the outdoors.

3. Family Art Project: Find an online art tutorial and have the whole family grab supplies and follow along. Then host an art show for the family with everyone's work of art.

4. Cooking competition. Let everyone in the family create a simple dish with only ingredients that are already in the house. Have everyone taste test and then vote for their favorite, the craziest combination, and any other fun categories you can think up.

What are some ideas you can come up with? Choose one to do today:

_____

_____

_____

_____

Journal

You can let your thoughts flow freely, turn a verse into a prayer, or make a list of things that bother you and you want to talk to God about.
Use this page however you like.

_____

_____

_____

_____

_____

_____

_____

_____

_____

_____

_____

_____

_____

_____

_____

_____

Monthly Reflection

As each month unfolds in your amazing adventure with Lectio Divina, taking time to think about what you've learned becomes super important for growing spiritually. This monthly review is like a chance to pause and think about your journey. Think about the words and Bible verses that meant the most to you and how they connect with your life - the good stuff, the challenges, and the happy moments. When you look back at your journal and think about your special times of thinking, here are some questions to help:

1. What Did You Like Most: Think about the Bible verses that meant the most to you this month. Why did you like them so much?

2. Any Big Ideas: Did you notice any big ideas or messages that kept coming up when you were reading? How do they connect to what's happening in your life?

3. What Did God Teach You: What did you learn from God as you read and thought about those special words?

4. How Did You Change: Did you feel different in your heart or thoughts this month because of what you learned from Lectio Divina?

5. Plans for Next Time: Based on what you've learned, what do you want to do or learn more about in the next month with Lectio Divina?

This monthly review helps you see how you're growing, how you're getting closer to God, and how the words from the Bible are guiding you. It's like a map for your journey of learning and growing with Lectio Divina!

_____

_____

_____

_____

_____

Monthly Reflection

_____

_____

_____

_____

_____

_____

_____

_____

_____

_____

_____

_____

_____

_____

_____

_____

_____

From Reflection to Action:
Translating Lectio Divina Insights into Daily Practice

It's time to turn the lessons you've learned into actions that can make the world a better place:

Truly I tell you, whatever you did for one of the least of these brothers and sisters of mine, you did for me."

Matthew 25:40 (NIV)

☐ Volunteer

☐ Give

☐ Share what you've learned

☐ Connect with friends

☐ Inspire someone

- Consider committing to a way to implement one of these into your life
- Brainstorm ideas of how you will put this into action
- List names of friends with whom you want to share what you've learned
- Once you've taken action, journal about the experience

Perfume and incense bring joy to the heart, and the pleasantness of a friend springs from their heartfelt advice.

Proverbs 27:9 (NIV)

Journal

You can let your thoughts flow freely, turn a verse into a prayer, or make a list of things that bother you and you want to talk to God about.
Use this page however you like.

_____

_____

_____

_____

_____

_____

_____

_____

_____

_____

_____

_____

_____

_____

_____

_____

Artistic Prompts

Artistic Prompts

Select one of these prompts to inspire your meditative art:

1. **Nature's Symphony:** Draw or paint your favorite season and the sounds you imagine in nature during that time.

2. **Imagine a New World:** Create a colorful and imaginative map of a world you'd like to explore, with magical creatures and hidden treasures.

3. **Animal Adventure:** Draw an animal you love and imagine a day in its life, from morning to night.

4. **Dreamy Doodles:** Make a page full of swirls, doodles, and patterns in your favorite colors.

5. **My Superhero:** Design your very own superhero with unique powers and a cool costume.

6. **A Splash of Emotions:** Use colors and shapes to express different emotions like happiness, sadness, excitement, and calmness on a single page.

7. **Under the Sea:** Create an underwater scene with colorful fish, coral, and maybe even a friendly mermaid or merman.

8. **My Dream Treehouse:** Draw your dream treehouse and all the fun things you'd have inside it.

9. **Invent a New Planet:** Imagine a planet with unusual creatures, landscapes, and plants. Show us what it looks like.

10. **Travel Journal:** Design a page that looks like a journal entry about a place you'd love to visit someday. Write about what you'd do and see there.

PatternIdeas

Select 2-4 patterns to create your own meditative artwork piece:

PatternIdeas

Select 2-4 patterns to create your own meditative artwork piece:

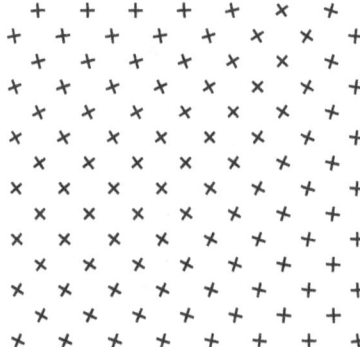

PatternIdeas

Select 2-4 patterns to create your own meditative artwork piece:

A Heartfelt Thank You

As we come to the end of this special journey together, I want to say a big thank you to you, my wonderful reader. Thanks for being brave and trying something new, for wanting to get closer to God, and for letting me be your guide. Your curiosity and determination on this journey have meant a lot to me. I hope you've found peace, inspiration, and a strong connection with God in these pages. Remember, your journey is special and just for you, and I feel really lucky to have been part of it. As you keep exploring and growing spiritually, may the peace, love, and wisdom you've found here be with you every step of the way on your amazing journey ahead.

♡ Samara

ways for Parents to Connect

f Join our FB group for community support, Serene Sketches videos, and additional artistic prompts.
Still Waters & Abiding Peace

SCAN ME

⊡ Share your Lectio Divina Journey and Tag us:
Still Waters & Abiding Peace
@SW.and.AP

Devo with your Parents

We've created this journal for kids, but we've also created a journal for parents too! If your parent doesn't have their own journal yet, you can ask them to check out the parent's version and they can join along in the journey!

Have your parent check out our FB Group and IG page for more info on how to get the adult journal for your family.

Made in United States
Cleveland, OH
14 June 2025